# this is my awakening.

**Mia Gutierrez**

ANGELENA MIA GUTIERREZ

AWAKENING

# THIS IS MY
# AWAKENING

THIS IS MY

AWAKENING

THIS IS MY

AWAKENING

THIS IS MY

for the children of the light
who are anxious and troubled
about many things
but only
**one thing**
is
necessary.

to those who choose the good portion,
it **will not** be taken away from them.

# foreword.

**What this book is about.** The truth is, when Jesus saves its a process not an overnight change. There's a salvation that does happen in a blink of an eye. You were once we against God, and now you stand covered in the blood of Jesus and justified before the throne. This is not what this book is about.

This book is about sanctification. What happens after you respond to the calling God has over your life? We are constantly being transformed from one degree of glory to another with unveiled eyes (2 Corinthians 3:18).

I found this process feels more like a cycle instead of linear progress. Instead of constantly moving forward and backward, I feel myself going around and around in an upward spiral. Like a caterpillar that gives way to 'dying' so that his new, glorified life may begin, except instead of once, it keeps occuring in different areas of my life.

This book was being manifested for four years. I felt like I was dying but God was bringing me to a point where a new degree of holiness and faithfulness to him could abound.

Christians undergoing the process of sanctification are constantly in the process of falling asleep and becoming awake again. The glorious thing is that when awake from a dry spell, we awake more and more alive each time God brings us back. Each time he takes us back to the simplicity of the gospel and the Gospel becomes sweeter and sweeter.

———

**The illustrations in this book** are original artwork and are visual representations of how I felt at each stage in this process of coming awake again.

———

**Now I will tell you about the process of the book.** When I began this book it was like a life line had been severed and I was bleeding everywhere on these pages. I'll be more specific. I accepted Christ into my life my Junior Year of Highschool. My sohopmore year of college I chased after the things of this world. When a relationship that had become the heartbeat of my world, collapsed, everything went with it. I was brought close to formlessness. Everything was as if God had never touched it in Genesis. It was choas, and darkness and void. My trust in everyone was nonexistent. There was no longer any purpose. It was as if God was a shooting star that lit up my world for two years and all went black.

The beginning of this book is drenched in the darkness of the consequences of me turning to everything and anything but God to feel alive again.

**I had sold my soul for that which was not bread. I felt dead in my sin, like I had tasted all the goodness of God one was alloted to recieve.**

I began this book officially after a poetry jam night at The Coffeehouse at Chesnut and Pine on October 18th, 2018. Even at this point, I was still dabbling in texts and phone calls from my ex and struggling to choose Jesus wholeheartedly again.

**This book you are holding in your hands, is the wrestling mat between me and God.**

I want to be honest about that and who I was when I wrote this book. I thought about adding so much more wisdom and victory now that I am past the heartache, but I felt like it would have done this honest, raw process a disservice. I would have felt as if I was tricking you, reader, if I wrote in this book from a healed place. It would have tainted the truth with false pretense. I realized that healed truth is for another seperate book entirely. What you are about to read is me in utter darkness, and waking to life again. There are many things I am not proud of, but I won't edit it out. God doesn't save perfect people, he saves broken people. God has replaced my shame of past events with perfect love, as he does with all his daughters and sons.

I write this foreward with a whole heart surrendered and a steady pace on the ancient paths, where the good way is, walking in it. I write this foreward with scabs and deep scars from my past that shine in the sunlight of truth. I'm encouraged by this because even my Savior has scars he will show me one day. He and his children were and are meant to feel a pain that gives life to genuine love and freedom. **Mind you, without Jesus, pain is pointless and senseless.**
I pray that you find safety, assurance of salvation, rest for your weary soul, and a recommitted life to Christ within these pages, as I did.

   grace & peace
   - mia g.

# list of illustrations

this book is the window to a struggling soul
i felt like i had pressed into Jesus as far as i could go
and met a dead end
this book is about my *coming to life* again

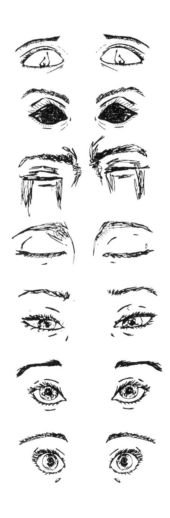

Love is your favorite oppressor,
you have learned to flaunt It's chains,
learned to close your eyes &
made your peace in falling away.
Only Grace, slipping like small sunlight
underneath your dungeon door,
can strip you of everything &
give freedom like never before.


- mia g.

The quickening of my heartbeat
running a mile
the sandpaper of my tongue
like you haven't kissed me right
in a while
the shaking of my hands
because you've been so cold
I got that car-wreck
gut-wrench feeling
before I saw her name on
your phone.
Before the mind thinks to calculate,
before the heart dares to speculate,
the body knows.

- mia g.

Falling leaves
shake you and me
winter wind gives you cold feet.
Summer sweeps
you back and then
a new thought blooms in me.

I won't ever control the weather
& these faithful, lonely Novembers
have taught me how to unremember
my need of you.

- mia g.

You are a cursed blessing.
It's not a compliment when I say
you are ungodly good at possessing.

Demonic powers which make
me a stranger to my own soul
& when I rebuke you,
I feel even more alone.

It was naive to believe
inviting an evil spirit into me
means I control when it comes
and when it leaves.

- mia g.

Every false hope must fall through
until you realize
a man can't rescue you
from that which he cannot see,
he could never feed your soul
by fixing circumstances
instead of their problems underneath.
Be careful when your prayers
begin to turn into pleas
for a mere human to do
the task of an infinite being,
know you are asking for
a candle to light the night sky,
& the darkness will win over you,
and you will wonder why.

- mia g.

This isn't love
Still clinging to memories
of the first sweet months.
When you were trying your hardest
to put up a front
of who you thought
I wanted you to be
And the entire time
I was unashamedly me
When did it stop being enough?
This isn't love.
I have to watch my own back,
trust you or I'm the problem,
though you've lied so much in the past.
Love doesn't do wrong
because it knows I will forgive anyway
It doesn't take advantage of my desperate
desire to believe every word you say.
Why does my connection to you
feel like bondage I can't rid myself of?
This isn't love.

- mia g.

Today
is a sick day.

I am sick of finally falling asleep
and hearing my alarm clock sound off.
I am sick of laying myself
down for others to walk across
I am sick of forcing inspiration
and personal hopes falling through
I am sick of waking up
to endless things I have to do.

Today
is a sick day
& I refuse
to keep going through the motions
just because the world expects me to.

- mia g.

Yesterday
is my favorite
way to remember you,
but Paul McCartney
will never sing it
like you used to.

- mia g.

Staring in the face of failure
another shut door
my initial reaction
is not to try anymore.

- mia g.

Your idea of love
made me crack
like pressing slowly &
strongly against thin glass.
My spirit broken,
like an icicle
falling
fast.
I hit the cruel, glittering pavement
and melted in the shadow
you cast.

- mia g.

I don't want to be the sad girl anymore
I don't want to make a big deal
how can I become cold and callous
and numb to everything I feel?
I burned your pictures and
smashed the painting I made you
and still no release.

How come you still get all of me?

- mia g.

steady as the flowers
we grow,
steady as the morning
we know,
a brighter day is coming.

- mia g.

bloodshot eyes
sleep wont fix
she sits still as
patience
turns to
hopelessness
but I promise you, dear
you won't recognize
the sad girl you've become
come this time
next year.

- mia g.

The only thing we have left in common now
is that we are both lonely.

- mia g.

Silence used to be
water to help me grow
and now I'm afraid of

It

Makes me feel alone.

- mia g.

You are a closed door
a haunting dial tone
that has no record
of who you were before.
You are a cut cord
and can't go home
the way you came,
settling in an empty house,
hoping it will be the same.


- mia g.

My heart feels unworthy
to look upon real grief
all the heartbreaks I've ever had
have been caused by me.

- mia g.

Hope, you are just like him,
knocking at my door,
promising things will be different
like you've promised a thousand times before.

And I've never turned you away,
my heart has always believed in the good,
eager to trust you again,
but this time, I just don't believe I could.

Hope, I want you to understand
all your lessons haven't been
pointless.
I've finally learned to accept
trusting you is just
delayed disappointment.

*absence of truth* | mia g.

(inspired by Tara Condell)

Longing for my company
while you lie awake in her bed
you thought you were betraying me
but betrayed yourself instead.

- mia g.

I used to love
my dark paradise
wrapped in the night
until you revealed
how it looked
in the light.

- mia g.

I'm falling asleep
to my favorite songs
but you've sung them so much
the love of them is gone
I can only hear your voice singing
my music vividly
sounds like you robbing
myself of me.

- mia g.

Go ahead
and show everyone
how better off you
acted like you would be
without him.

*I'm my own worst enemy* | mia g.

I'm too hurt to understand why
you did what you did
maybe one day I will have the
grace to ask and not let your answer wreck me
or maybe I'll never get over it.

- mia g.

You are not a dumb girl
for the thousands of times you've run back
into his hurting hands.
Love in it's most manipulated form
is hard for outsiders
to understand.
Toxic relationships are
revolving doors,
only you can decide when
you want to leave yours.

- mia g.

Maybe we worship the past
and lust for the future
because it's forbidden fruit we can't touch.
The overwhelming potential of the present
is what makes us afraid
and hate it so much.

*the present is the closest we get to eternity* | mia g.

Our love made us both blind
we thought the worst days were behind us
but our unlove is worse and has pushed us both
further into blindness.

- mia g.

she uproots all the ways you have grown
she unplants budding seeds
she doesn't need you to say sorry
she doesn't believe in apologies
she says the darkness is light
she teaches you to unsee
& you like her for all the ways she is wrong for you
because then she'll never remind you of me.

- mia g.

Though I fought it the whole way,
you ended up being who you were all along
and when you were gone,
I wondered why being you was such a bad thing
and they fell hard upon my head like pattering rain
all the times I had been wrong.

- mia g.

I resented you for
being nothing
when you made me feel like
I was everything.
How easy it was to pick you apart
when you gave me your whole heart
on a silver platter & fed it to me.

- mia g.

You helped keep me helpless
for so long
Now I'm without you
I realize the strong
are only truly strong
because they have to be
& at the end of the day
the only one who has to deal
with my decisions
is me.

- mia g.

I love to say big things
to free me of feeling small
some days I wish I had done it better from the start
some days I don't think it would have made a
difference at all
irreversible actions
that feel meant to happen
& all the building we did together
was just circumstantial.


- mia g.

Some nights
I feel perfectly insane
my mind keeps talking in poetry
as I stare at my bedroom ceiling
listening to the short circuits
in my brain
fill the silence with irritable humming
I accidentally rub leftover makeup
in my eye and think of what I'm becoming
I won't have what it takes to keep drumming
out this poetry.

I don't know what to do with me.


- mia g.

Anytime a desire becomes a desperation
it will always be abused.
Every love that is clung to
will always be misused.

- mia g.

A person
by believing a lie
shuts themselves up
smaller and smaller inside
until they have no ears to hear
and no eyes to see
and they reverse time
by becoming
unborne,
still and lifeless.

*true sadness* | mia g.

Hearts crumple like drafts
of a frustrated writer
i want to
rewrite
rewrite
rewrite
the names I have
written,
I've wasted
so much
paper.

- mia g.

Your peace is too high a price
to advertise and sell
selling peace is the severing
of flesh and spirit
like a stolen pearl
& an empty oyster shell.

- mia g.

I'm sorry I left us desperate and numb,
me and you both
don't know the thing you have become.

- mia g.

You said I shouldn't get bent out of shape
about mistakes and right and wrong.
I greedily accepted the sweet release
from being a good girl too long
and lived in free
rebellion towards a deity
that had always protected me
from becoming the worst I could be.

You taught me your empty truths,
I became more and more like you
because you swore it would make us closer
& it wasn't until after that I knew
when you pick a flower from its field
its beauty doesn't last long
before the new state is revealed
I had been uprooted in vain
when I withered you were disgusted
as my darknesses became
more like you looking in the mirror
and me and you became the same


When my light you so loved burned out
you left me in the darkness you created
dealing with the unlovable parts of myself
that reflected the parts of yourself that you hated

while you hungrily searched
to find something just as bright
as the girl that brought sunrise to your darkness,
the girl you had sacrificed to the night.

- mia g.

Treating yourself
is spending time
& money
building a life
you don't have to
run away from
instead of incurring
emotional debt
distracting yourself
until the next
paycheck comes.

- mia g.

My biggest fear
is not being able to break through
your suffocating loneliness
while sitting right beside you.

- mia g.

I can't stop
thinking about my dad
leaning against the kitchen sink
his overalls have holes
from his welding.
his knuckles are cracked
from the Wisconsin cold,
His eyes are steady
and for the first time in a long time
I realize he is growing old.
his countenance is forever
observing &
his surveying eyes
begin unnerving
what I want him to see.
"You're settling," the words cut clean.
"What happened to your writing?
you spend all your time and energy
dwelling on a mistake
that you made momentarily.
what's two years compared to twenty two?
you have a whole life ahead of you.
don't let such a small mistake in the past
steal your future too."

*let it go* | mia g.

I tear open the box I saved for you
finally accepting things will never be the same
the cold frostbite on my toes burns
like the memories of you I toss in flames
I watch Polaroids of us smear in the smog
& wonder why are we born with the ability to reason
and an inability to know the meaning behind it all?
Now I know how the Devil feels
when he wants to set the whole world ablaze
Watching all the frustrating turmoil
(he can't understand)
melt away.

- mia g.

Sometimes we must
burn bridges
to forbid ourselves
from crawling back.
There was a reason
after gaining freedom
our safe sea canopy
back to Egypt
collapsed.

- mia g

Like a perfect bride left at the altar
we run away because we know we don't deserve her.

*second chances* | mia g.

*Want to grab coffee?*
it seems like a simple text
that deserves a simple answer
that I can't deliver
maybe if she genuinely just
wanted to see how I was doing
instead of question every
answer I give her
maybe if she used the gospel
as a candlelight to guide my way
instead of bright interrogation light
blinding, pure and harsh in my face
maybe if I didn't feel like she had an obligation
or secret agenda to convert me
I would say "of course, lets meet
here are some areas in my life that have been hurting."
Of course, I could say
"I am converted, I'm one of you"
but she wouldn't believe me
because my attendance isn't perfect
and my life doesn't look pretty like she wants it to.

- mia g.

We had both promised
not to let things go this far
Now I know how feeble
the promises of humans are
And a man can't control
a hair falling from his head
& the love that promised life to me
brought death to me instead.

*Godless love* | mia g.

I wish I could have loved you better
I wish I could have loved myself
enough for the both of us
I wish you had protected me
like you said you would
pull close the chasm between us
instead it gaped open like a bloody gash,
revealing true bones beneath

you were never really mine for eternity.

- mia g.

When I was angry and sad
you always knew what I wanted you to say
you knew just how I liked to be coddled
and how to give me my way
and that helped me become the monster
that I now fight alone to keep at bay
and, oh, how she wallows in your empty words,
that never matched your actions at the end of the day.

- mia g.

Humans are half-spirit, half-animal
our bodies are forced to inhabit time
while our souls dwell in matters of the eternal

The animal in me craves
things and people that constantly change
but my spirit won't let me settle in the ephermeral.

- mia g.

God, you have always led me
in the way I should go
by every door that slammed in my face
every time you told me no
I hated you for it
because I didn't truly know
life is not a living body
it's a living soul.

*you were ressurecting me* | mia g.

I am no longer afraid of the silence
in the quiet you speak
I remember when darkness was blindness
until you taught my soul to see.

- mia g.

Pressing into the soft spots of the heart,
kneading into them like dough,
forgetting for a moment the
anxious currents in undertow.

I can finally see you across from me.
A living, breathing beast,
with an animal craving and human need
to be loved and known platonically.

*the art of self-forgetfulness* | mia g.

Let me sleep, I'm tired of my grief
I would like you to love me
but your words hold such weak relief.

I beg for your empty words
& I desperately try to believe
let me sleep, I'm tired of my grief.

Lies have to be consistent to breed unbelief
your poisoned lips kissed this realization upon me
now your words have become weak relief.

A cocktail of lies and truth make my behavior spin
and my forgiveness brief
let me sleep, I'm tired of my grief.

When I get what I want most,
you turn to gravel between my teeth
my cluttered mind overflows with truth I can't unsee
and your excuses hold weak relief
I offered my heart to your sword
as a cursed stoned sheath
the wound will remain solidified, unyielding
until the rightful king promised to me.

For now, let me sleep I'm tired of this grief.
because of you I've lost my faith in words,
once my fortress of relief.

- mia g.

Faith does not create realities,
it recognizes realities God has made.
Faith realizes everything infront of my eyes is
temporary and bound to fade.
The energy of faith is seeking, it fixes forward our gaze
to see to Sun on the horizon, and lets its light guide our way.

Faith belongs to those who have
been pierced with an infinite desire.
It's having unquenchable thirst
like a body of wildfire.

Faith knows no turning back
it is bound by a desire for the homeland.
Faith never tarries in one city too long
lest the ground give way to quicksand.

First the cross, then the crown
first the pilgramage, then the promised ground.
Faith knows what it leaves behind is dust
because it knows the one who has promised us.

- mia g.

*Shout out to Spencer Deburgh! Favorite Pastor of all time! This poem is based of his sermon "By Faith" during his million year series on Hebrews (Okay, it was really probably only a year but it was very long -- which, was obviously very good for my soul).

When I thought you had forsaken me
you were beginning my awakening
how pain staking
to look back and
see the foundation of who I was shaking
like a dead autumn leaf
a younger version of me,
lonely in his bedroom,
tears rolling off my cheek
soaking into the complacent soft, silk sheets
I can remember the paralyzing fear
like I was screaming inside a glass box,
and everyone saw me but
no one could hear.

- mia g.

and greatest offense was this
that I turned to your creation
to get what only you can give

and my greatest sin was this
everything you said would hurt me
I held tightly in my fist.

*pain, confusion, error* | mia g.

I cant believe it took me this long
to realize the decision I made to leave you
wasn't a reaction to your wrongs
but a decision I would have made all along.

*decisions we make are a projection*
*of what's going on inside of us,*
*not outside of us* | mia g.

We live life between
the moon and the sun,
between doing what's right
to cover up wrong we have done.

Our spirits are torn
between ground and flight,
married to darkness
while lusting for the light.

We are a momentary eclipse,
an astrological, star-crossed kiss —
but the equinox is coming
when you will be what you are now becoming.

- mia g.

When she is
threatening in your eyes
you decide
she is nothing special.
Based on the way
she thrives,
you decide
the way she would judge
your own personal issues.
Putting your own insecurities
on her silent lips,
you misuse
the reason other humans exist —
not for comparison —
but to bring you out
of your contagious
darknesses.

- mia g.

I think frantically
in poetry
insomnia
is my nightly liturgy
knowing there is
eternity
interwoven in me
I can't seem
to get release
from this constraining
mortality.

- mia g.

I want to be a prophetess
casting new visions of ancient belief
advocating for the spirit
in people who long to see
Hope
as it was originally
without man-made laws and limitations
without all these negative "christian" connotations
I want to preach truth,
and the truth I preach is this:

Though you are poor in spirit,
if you lift up the broken hearted within your reach
you will see
there is far more growth
in the planter
than the soil in which they
plant the seed.

- mia g.

Women are the reason
you exist
we are the pillars that hold up
a culture knocking us down
& if we give in to every
kick
humanity wouldn't persist.

*she persists, we persist* | mia g.

Instead of becoming
a monument of
mortal tragedy,
the treasure beneath
my fragility
was heavenly,
as buried light
began shining
from within me.

- mia g.

Being a humanist
does not mean
loving the broken shards of
imperfections stuck
like thrones in your soul
which prevent you from being
who you want to be

It's more than
exploring the human state
and describing our depravity
I am more concerned
in restoring
what humans were intended to be
in all their original glory.

- mia g.

Why must I write about your toxicity
in order for you to like
what I'm saying?
Why do I need to glorify what enslaves you?
To make beautiful
what breaks you?
I will not exalt what kicks you down.
But I will write
in stone
what keeps your spirit sound.


- mia g.

The Bride of Blessing
flat-nosed, dark skin & almond eyes
a girl's desperation to hide
& a woman's crown of pride.

- mia g.

Ugliness exists to magnify Beauty,
Darkness is defined by the absence of Light,
what the eyes of your soul are seeking
is found by faith and not by sight.

- mia g.

I used to long for your
lies to lull
the convictions of
my spirit to sleep.
Now I desire
a new way to dream,
sinking into melodies of truth
oceans deep.

- mia g.

The evil presence in my life
wasn't a human
suffocating me.
The evil was
internalized lies
I had let myself believe.
Lies that told me
it is selfish to want
to be free.

- mia g.

Out of all truths,
this is most frustrating—
doing the right thing
doesn't guarantee blessing.

Sacrifice never promises
She will give you back tenfold,
& if Dignity is fought for,
itself is the reward.

So we press on &
wage war
for the sake of
Goodness
and nothing more.


- mia g.

There are times
when my heart, body and mind
align with God's will for my life
like an astrological sign
in
the
night.
These moments are what it feels like
to touch the sky.

*running, praying, worshiping* | mia g.

Knowing God runs deep,
appropriate, good and fitting.
it's like marrying someone, and then realizing
the moment you met them you were committing.

Knowing God
satisfies like a puzzle piece snapping into place
like fingertips intertwining
like a runners footsteps steadily paced.

Knowing God
is to be drenched in love's fullness
soaking of his goodness
a melting heart dripping grace.

- mia g.

Let me remain here
earthed, planted, grounded
like a tree whose roots run deep
remaining in your house forever
as your words fall into the soft soil of my heart
like rain, they seep.
Then, I can see your goodness all my days.
Then, my soul knows where to find you always.

- mia g.

A cloud overshadows me
and I know this is holy ground
it leaves and I know nothing
but to follow you around
you gathered me close to you in the wilderness
like a motherless lamb
you saved me from wild wolves
and fed me straight from your hand.
and taught me to trail clumsily after you,
taught me the heart behind doing good,
and how to love complete strangers
as their own family would.
I am a wanderer now for all of this life
and someone who doesn't know you
wouldn't think it right
to chase corners of your robe
because they don't know that chasing your shadow
is the closest we get to home.

*tabernacle* | mia g.

There are nights
I prayed for you to
numb and harden my heart.
How does one pray
to the God of life
to deaden every part?

- mia g.

Sleepy lavender eyelids,
coffee stains on my wooden workspace
saran wrapped in my mom's high school t-shirt
comfortably cross-legged in my messy place.

this moment is like a sponge
soaking silence.

- mia g.

Let the thief no longer steal
driven by his desires
he knows not deceive him.
Instead let his anxiousness drive
him to fruitfulness
from within
and see that instead of taking
giving all he can give
fulfills the need of his.

- mia g.

the resurrected life
is hard to live
because it means dying everyday
to every evil we must unlive.

- mia g.

I used to leave the door open
to my house of bricks
for everyone to enjoy
the saving sturdiness.

I used to take the long way home
over the river and through the woods
stopping to pick peonies and help
a lost stranger if I could.

That was before,
when the big bad wolf
was just a children's lore
now I know a tale of a monster could not be told
unless someone had seen it before.

and once I saw his face
I could not unsee it in every boy
that wanted to swallow me whole
and snuff out every joy.

So I sealed my house of bricks
behind a double bolted door,
like the submerged city of Atlantis,
I won't give away my gifts anymore.

- mia g.

My little lamb,
you bound through life
with such a
      clumsy
 passion.
Oh, the thing you could be
If I molded and shaped you
in wisdom, to
direct
your
action.


*how much more will hasty feet miss the way* | mia g.

Love's work is never done.
I wake up in the morning
to golden beams of a hardworking sun
urging me to wake up too,
urging me to prove
love is an action that we do.

- mia g.

I wake up from a nightmare
no human can save me from
I can't expect a hero to ride in
at every battle that comes.
So I start my day early
with a hot pot of coffee
& pour myself some,
and I head ouside to pull weeds,
and my nightmare
melts
    in the
        morning
            sun.

- mia g.

God and you come first
anyone from the past that made you sad
dwelling on them just makes it worse.
consider the walk to where you are now
did you know then you had won?
No, you don't know until you get to the next fight
that the last battle is overcome.
I know you feel like giving up,
don't you think some days, I do too?
But the thing is everyone feels these waves
You're not doing this just for you
if you cave, we all cave
you don't carry your cross for yourself
when you carry it, other people get saved.
remember—you're doing this for all of us.
remember—you're doing this for me.
everytime you choose God, it'll have a ripple effect,
maybe you'll never get to fully see.
Your faith is a stepping stone for us all
and if you forget why you're doing this again,
just give me a call.

*phone call from my little brother* | mia g.

When I put it in gear, the whole thing rocks back and forth
like we're deep-sea fishing and I'm going to be sick
thinking of the long line of cars behind me,
I give the clutch a quick kick.
Dad shouts as we rumble into traffic,
"Just press the brake!"
I stomp on the brake & it throws me against the wheel
I bite my tongue for both of our sakes.
I throw it into gear,
and do a half-hearted scan
*this is so simple, just do it,* I yell in my head,
*stop being a baby and do it! I know you can!*
We lurch forward,
I thank God I didn't put it in reverse.
I press the gas harder to get out of traffic first
but the gas just makes the rocking worse

I start over again by squeezing the brake
"This time don't dump the clutch,"
I get angry at every suggestion he makes.
I imagine taking my foot off every peddle
and letting it all kill
saying, *fine you just drive it*
but the line of cars is growing still
so ease slowly off the clutch,

still feeling like I'm going to throw up
and press the gas down lightly at the same time
I'm almost angry this time it starts off just fine.
instead of going home,
my dad makes me chug around the block,
he answers a phone call and is unable
to help me at stopsign when we stop.
I have chop along until I figure it out
it's hard the whole way,
I almost start crying
when we're back in our driveway.

I choke it back, ready to get yelled at with dignity
press the parking brake in
we both listen to the sweet sound of air brake release
and dad has the audicity
to turn to me from the passenger seat
with a smile and says
"See, now wasn't that easy?"

*learning to drive a gravel truck* | mia g.

Thank God for sisters,
because of them I have three open clothes racks
even when I gained a lot weight
they let me wear their clothes until
they wouldn't stretch back.
Then, they took me to the gym
and we got hype to the Jon Bellion soundtrack.

They showed me how fun getting fit could be
and binge watched my favorite tv series
so they could watch the season finale with me.

All of these tiny little testimonies show me
my sisters would never withold any good thing
not even Chipotle,
when all I had was a dollar thirty three
and all along these funny, little memories
are what God used to redeem me.

*I love my sisters* | mia g.

daughter of real love,
twenty is old enough to go to war,
you shine light in places that have never
been touched by goodness before.

- mia g.

The effects of accessible prayer
are just insidious.
because it should make us pray more
but instead it makes us prayerless.


- mia g.

Free me of breaking my own heart, God
I pray to have power over emotions
help me to stop giving into lies
and self-deprecating notions.
they create panic that separates me from you,
they paralyze me from loving others,
which is what the enemy
exactly wants to do.
make me believe,
you will make no way for me to get through
and I'm at the mercy of other people
to give me value.
What a fearful thing it is
to fall into the hands of man
to think it's your responsibility
to make life turn out right
is to doubt that God can.

*pray more, stress less* | mia g.

It suprised me how much I adored
The scar like a shooting star
stretching across your hardworking hand.
It seemed as if we were both naturally adorned
with little attributes meant to draw eachother in
like how your shirts smelled like my dads machine shop
I used to run around in as a kid
and how you loved my long, dark hair
because I represented a wholesome culture
you finally felt peace within.

You taught me wordly wisdom and how to
appreciate every moment
even when it didn't go my way.
You taught me that I didn't always need my words
and sometimes sitting with someone in silence
speaks in ways words can't say.

You taught me that if a man really loves a woman
he actually prefers the wait,
he fights to keep her preserved
and protects the integrity she radiates.

You were the first man I met too kind
to pick a flower for beauty's sake,
you understand the thing that keeps her beautiful
are the roots reaching deep in faith.

& when you played Stevie Nicks on your record player
I closed my eyes and thought how easy it was for you to be good
and how easy it was for you to make me fall in love again
when I thought I never could.

*falling for you, pt. 1* | mia g.

It's a misconception,
to believe it's in anyone's nature to do good.
There is a difference between choosing goodness and
desiring goodness because you know you should.

When we laid on the floor in your room
and talked until midnight, I assumed
you were just taking a little longer
to bloom.

You made it seem like you desired Goodness as much as me
but I knew you didn't know Him by name
because for all the good you did, you wanted His glory
and talked as if falling in love & cultivating it
were the same.

I tried to tell you
but you hated to hear me
it's not enough to live for yourself
and stumble upon moments of beauty
true beauty is a call to action,
not a feeling of appreciation
this is when you refused to understand
& drowned in the depth of our conversation.

we all have dark parts we need grace for,

but I see now it was my light you would not endure
It was an inconvience to you
to have conversations with a 'complicated' girl.
What was so complicated?
Who I am? Or the way it makes you feel intimidated?
Was it when I peeled the scales off your eyes
that you became so frusterated?

I tried to unviel your eyes
I tried to set you free
now I've learned my lesson
It's not my job to make the blind see
& sometimes men hide behind masks so long
even they are fooled by who they want themselves to be.

I chose to dive in the deep &
it's your choice to not make a choice
instead you sweep
the shore, admiring those who do
You pitched your tent at the fork in the road,
and I must continue on without you.

*falling for you, pt. 2* | mia g.

I'm going into another valley,
I can feel my spirit plummeting
I can see below me,
the vast darkness summoning.

It knows me by name
know which daydreams are my favorite
to make me play Pain's game
I hate the darkness edging out goodness in me

I'm the victim and a wolfpack of old sin
nipping at me from all sides to weary me before it attacks
her side glares, her impatience, her cursing—
my old self, she's coming back.

- mia g.

I don't have the capacity to hold sadness
I'm a sinking boat
Now I understand why I push myself down,
it's the only way I know how to float.

- mia g.

The chaos of me glassy eyed and fighting
is a bar filled with fake fellowship and backsliding
Why did you open my eye
to all the damage I thought I left behind
flaring up memories I had forgotten
as a way of coping with a 'complicated' mind

and so a test becomes temptation because
I'm not as strong as I thought I was.

- mia g.

Alcohol loosens the dam between my
heart and my lips.

- mia g.

On a sunday morning
I'll douse myself in a hot shower,
hoping to wash Saturday night sins away
like the city water tank is filled with holy water.

- mia g.

The whole point of being Christian
is knowing truth
and the truth freeing you of the control
fickle emotions have over you.

What good is having all the wisdom
I need to conquer the day,
if it's never enough to free me
from my emotions controlling what I say?

- mia g.

God pours out
his own being
into us and makes all that is.

Although we
create like he creates,
our work is in opposition.

we unmake what God makes
until he pours himself out again.

- mia g.

Bitterness is a crown of thorns
I pridefully press against my own forehead.
The sovereignty You meant to give me hope,
has made me resent You instead.

If You're the one in control, I still can't understand
why did things happened the way they did.
Behind a blinding cloud of corruption,
your true character is hid.

In this momentary darkness, I am cast into confusion
and maybe the only consolation that will be understood
are small byproducts of a bad situation
that you continue to use for good.

*we are not called to understand his ways,*
*we are called to obey his ways* | mia g.

Loving you was like looking in the mirror
Why did I choose you?
What parts of me are broken here?

*"What's wrong in you, that you keep*
*choosing these kind of guys?"* | mia g.

I know how this process goes
I've been broken from bondage before
First I try forcing the brass handles,
until I remember I'm called to walk past a locked door.

I swim deep
to the dark parts of the soul
but instead hitting the rock bottom
I keep finding myself more and more.

I have to remind myself that I know
what I have to do to continue to grow
and fear is just a wave that passes over the surface
it's not scary to grow alone.

- mia g.

I have courage now
to ask if I understood you correctly
I am okay with being percieved as 'complicated'
as long as I made sure of the truth by asking directly.
I know now it doesn't matter what you think of me
regardless of what you believe,
I know who God says I am and I will continue to be.
I am a light in the darkness
I was born to obliterate confusion.
to yeild communication as a weapon
to defeat enslaving illusions.
Including the ones you are hiding behind.
I can break all your barriers down
only using my mind.
And I'll admit at first,
seeing a phantom was hard
but I have courage now
& I know exactly what you are.

*"fear is just a liar running out of breath"* | mia g.

I am sorry I used my power of words
to say things I didn't mean,
giving life to something make-believe,
instead of showing you the real me
even if she's someone you didn't find lovely.

*I am not always right* | mia g.

let me accept things for what they are
instead of dissapointed for what
they could be.
Let me rest in the fact you have
appointed a time for love,
and a time for understanding.
Let me not grow weary
of being mistreated
or others rejecting me.
I know its you in me
that they have seen &
they were not ready.

*luke 10:16* | mia g.

I am what I am
because you have made me so,
not to impress others
but to be a home wanderers go
when they cry out for truth
they find me to find you.
And that's something I can't change
you've given me a new name.

*safehouse for the gospel* | mia g.

leave every person as happy as you find them
find good words that give life
and rhyme them
make them fun to say,
say them goofy or silly, in a memorable way
sing them to children
and they'll sing them all day
they'll show all their friends
and their friend's friends
will all sing as they play
and your words won't come back empty,
instead of one happy person
there'll be plenty.

*I admire Shel Silverstein* | mia g.

People must belive what they can.
progress is progress,
and those who progress more
should not punish those who progress less.

- mia g.

Some people will say
she believes it, because its what she was taught
but I can't help believing
whether you do or not.

- mia g.

My sister is like rosewater
and salve
to a cracking soul.
When you are feeling
like you can't make it another day,
she knows exactly where to go.
On a lonely back road,
she always takes the scenice routes,
forty minutes away to a cozy coffeehouse
no one else would know about.
She is the embodiement of Godly grace,
the kind you don't deserve.
She knows all your favorite songs,
she sings along to your favorite verse.
She can light her flannel candle
and make any place feel like home
and she sacrifices herself for everyone
even on days she feels alone.

*Tessy* | mia g

Thick sheets of plywood,
we carry on our breaking backs
preparing for Wisconsin winters,
me and my dad work out back.
Always outside
pride pushed aside,
my dad teaches me
how to keep my mind occupied
until my only thought is how
to install a rubber roof
& when a car won't even click to start
he shows me what to do.
he teaches me
how to drive manual in a gravel truck,
& how to pull another quad axel
from the mud when it gets stuck.
how long to water a tree line
to make sure it grows,
& it's better to use a belt than chain
when someone's truck needs a tow.

He taught me to work fast,
but learn to live slow
 can never pay him back
for teaching me everything I know.

Like how to build my own shed.

I'm thankful for a dad that teaches me
how to put a roof over my own head.

*blue collar* | mia g.

When we suffer
we are tempted to believe,
God, you never cared
you don't even see me

but only those who make it past these moments
are those who will taste and see.

*he who promised is faithful* | mia g.

We can't decieve him with disquise.
God saved us with open eyes.

- mia g.

One of us has become
what we all shall be

and those ten words
are poetry.

*Jesus* | mia g.

The enemy has their hearts shackled
like caged doves
they become senile and senseless.
Everyday they become more irreversibly
defenseless.
against their slow transformation
from a human to mere animals
furthest from the first creation

Human souls can
when freed by christ
see what is in man
beyond the body they wear.

thank you, God, it was a part of your plan
to teach me how to discern
an animal from a man.

- mia g.

The heart is an idol making factory
I am thankful you reveal idolatry to me
before smashing it completely

the golden shards are glittering
before my child-like eyes
like mocking laughter

**I don't want your white-knuckled sacrifices,
its your heart I'm after.**

*turning over tables in my heart* | mia g.

You struck the rock that was my heart
and brought forth water
when it split apart
And the water
it filled it filled

and the rest of my dry bones sing,
"he will, he will."

- mia g .

The thought of you
makes me weep
all the angry mornings
and the nights we would fight instead of sleep
I wish I could take it back
undo the way I treated you
and show you all the things
a godly girlfriend can do

but that is a lie
I needed this
curtain ripped open wide
I needed to learn how to
truly apologize
I needed my idol of self-worship
smashed before my eyes

and it's a sweet sadness
that nothing ever happens
the same way twice, dear
but God has grown so much
goodness from our ashes that
my heart and conscience are clear.

*let go of godless guilt* | mia g.

it is a slow, low thing
to refuse to confess a fault
it is weak, bleak thing
to act as if it hadn't happened at all.
Even if you did it on an accident
it's not hard to admit it
"I wish I had not done it,
and I'm sorry that I did it."

*apologies give life to grace* | mia g.

## the woman at the well.

The scorching desert heat,
beating down hard against me
The hottest part of the day where
no other women would be.

I approach the well silently,
I see a man and I know he is a Jew
I know he will ignore me, maybe mock me
like all the rest of them do
I lower my jar into the well
and resolve to give him the silent treatment too.

I can tell he is tired, by way he is leaning
against the well so weak and so weary
"daughter, give me a drink,"
his voice is raspy and low
can he not see me clearly?

I stare him straight in the face
I forgot what I was going to say
the world around seemed to go dim
when he smiled at me that way

I remember who I am when I meet
his knowing eyes that make my heart sink

"If you knew who I was," I pause.
"You wouldn't ask me for a drink."

His lips are dry and cracked,
his eyes are an auburn hue
they are clear and they are blameless
but somehow open like window
as if they can see through.

He laughs low like soft thunder
and he gives me a wink
"if you knew who I was,
you would be the one asking me for a drink"

"You have nothing to draw with,"
is he mocking me now?
is this just another man who will rope me in
with empty promises and broken vows?
I won't allow myself to be taken in
is this a game he wants to play?
my heart falls to silence
hanging onto every word he had to say
"If you drink from this well
you will be thirsty again"
whoever drinks the water I give
will never have to send
their maidens and jars
to this well again."

This evil hungry spirit in me,
like a crow, constantly pecking
flew away in reckless abondon
I felt all darkness and lonliness melting.

"Sir, give me this water,"
I don't care if it is a trick
I need this to be true
and I need to have some of it.
I'm so sick of coming here to draw water
I'm so sick of refilling an empy jar
the walk is so shameful
and the well is so far

"First call your husband to come here,"
this was a trick
I wanted to dissapear
I almost forgot about who I was
the promise of new life had been so near.
"I have no husband"
I thought of him
who I'd left at home.
*Technically* he's not my husband
even though since we always sleep together,
& the Torah might say so.

"You are right about that,
you have had five husbands,"
the suddenly solemn Jew said
"And you're right about *technically*
not including the man who right now is
sleeping in your bed."

I've stood in front of what seems like
hundreds of men naked
and played their games
but I've never in my life felt
this vulnerable and ashamed.

Every dirty, unclean thing about me laid bare
I turned my face away,
"I perceive that you are a prophet,"
is the only thing I can bring myself to say.
Why did you have to come at this hour,
the hour I come to be lonely?
And promise to give living water
when all along you knew my story?
You are not shy,
unashamed, you keep looking at me
not my body, looking into who I am
as if there's something your waiting to see
I say, "I know my people are in the wrong,
we worship in the wrong place."

What I really am saying is
I know that **what I am is wrong** and
I cannot bear to look you in the face.

"It's not about the place you worship
it's about how you worship, my daughter
I tell you the truth, *and truth is the living water*
Very soon, people will not worship here or there
but in spirit and in truth and
they will worship anywhere."
I don't understand,
theology is something I never knew
I say, "well, the Messiah isn't here yet
until then, we won't know what to do."

He laughed again
fuller and livelier this time,
as if he had something to eat.
"Who do you think you've
been talking to all this time?
It's me -- I am he."

I dropped my clay jar
and it split in two
In that moment, my soul cried out
because it knew it was true.

A cluster of twelve men surrounded him
I hadn't heard them come
they sneered as if they wondered
"why are you talking with her?"
but I turned to run
I had never felt this way,
like they could talk about me all they wanted
& I didn't care what anyone had to say

My feet pounded as loud as my heart
and I didn't stop until the town drew near
To the first people I saw, I shouted
"Everyone! Can the Messiah really be here?
He's sitting right now at Jacob's Well!
from his eyes, nothing is hid!
He gave me living water
even though he knew everything I ever did!"

*the woman at the well pt. 1* | mia g.

I cry not because it's sad
but because God is good
I cry because I believed a lie
God wouldn't save me if he could
I cry because the devil got me to believe
that the things I did weren't wrong
but that the wrong thing was me
and if God knew what I did
he wouldn't call me redeemed.
But God
he is the reconciler and
he is the redeemer
That's just who he is!
He calls me beloved
even thought he knows
everything I ever did.
And its a joy to say I rememeber,
because it means it's in the past
I rememeber when I thought
the dark, dead night would forever last
I rememeber when darkness
like hell on me befell
I remember when I was
the woman at the well.

*the woman at the well pt. 2* | mia g.

even when we think
we are dead in our sleep
We are in the process of sleeping
and becoming awake constantly.
& when God brings us back,
we wake more alive each time
we are more complete
and the simplicity of the Gospel
becomes more sweet
and sweet.

God restores more than we can think to ask for

I am more awake now than I ever was before.

- mia g.

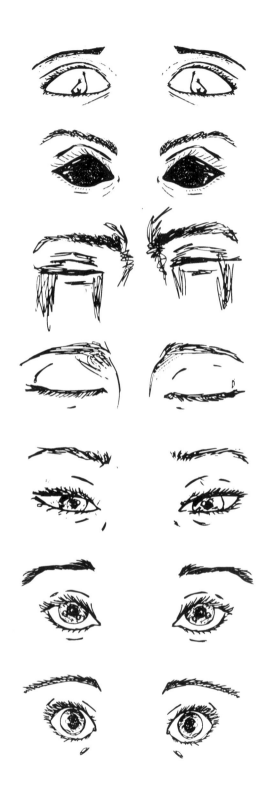

"The mind governed by the flesh is death,
but the mind governed by the Spirit is life
and peace."

Romans 8:6

# meet the author.

Mia Gutierrez went to school in Nashville, TN where she studied **English Language Arts at Belmont University.** She graduated in May 2018 and currently teaches Kindergarten at Hope Christian School. Among many creative things, Mia loves poetry, discovering new coffeshops, reading C.S. Lewis, and singing worship. She believes every moment is a new chance to start fresh and the key to happiness is living the abundant, ressurected life that comes with accepting Jesus.

Follow her blog at
**angelenamia.squarespace.com**
Instagram: angelena_mia

Made in the USA
Columbia, SC
13 August 2023

21549049R00085